About
Baptism

About Baptism

by

EMMA MARR PETERSEN

*A Story of
the Meaning and Purpose of
Baptism*

Bookcraft
Salt Lake City, Utah

1957

Lithographed in the United States of America
PUBLISHERS PRESS
Salt Lake City, Utah

CONTENTS

CHAPTER ONE

A New Home for Larry

"Hurry to bed now, Paul; you know the plane comes very early in the morning."

As his mother spoke, Paul Jensen looked up quickly and asked, "What time, Mother?"

"Seven o'clock," she said, "and that means we must get up at six, so go to bed at once."

Paul was excited. Tomorrow his cousin Larry would arrive from Denmark. Larry was going to make his home with Paul.

His name was really Lauritz, but that was hard for Paul to say, so he called him Larry.

Larry's father had been a Danish fisherman who went out on the sea to catch fish. When he had caught some, he sailed home and sold the fish, and in this way made a living. Sometimes he was gone for a week at a time. He loved the ocean, and that is why he chose fishing for his work. Larry loved the sea also, and hoped he could grow up and be a fisherman just like his dad.

But one day a bad storm came up while his father was fishing from his boat on the ocean. The boat sank in the

7

stormy sea and Larry's father was lost. From then on, Larry no longer liked the sea.

Larry's mother was a sister of Paul's mother. She and Larry were very poor after Larry's father died, and had to work hard to earn enough food to eat.

Larry was seven years old, the same age as Paul. He went with his mother to the fish market in Copenhagen where she worked every day. He helped too, when there were little jobs he could do.

One day Larry's mother became very sick, and soon she too died, leaving Larry an orphan. Kind friends took him into their home. They wrote to Sister Jensen, Paul's mother, asking what they should do about Larry, now that he had neither father nor mother.

The Jensens wrote back quickly and invited Larry to come to America and live with them, and be a pal to Paul. Larry was happy about this and so was Paul.

Paul wanted to write a letter to Larry to say how glad he was to have him come, but he could not speak or write Danish, and Larry could not read English. Paul's mother knew Danish, having been born in Denmark, so she wrote the letter and Paul signed it.

The missionaries helped Larry get ready for the trip. It was planned that he would come with one of the elders who had finished his mission and was returning to his home in America.

This was a great help to Larry, because a Danish boy traveling alone in America would find it very hard if he could speak no English.

Larry wanted to fly across the ocean in an airplane. He did not want to ride on a ship because he remembered too well the sinking of his father's boat.

At last the day came for them to leave Denmark. The missionaries and the Saints were there to say goodbye as they left the airport near Copenhagen. It was a great thrill for Larry when he stepped into the big plane and looked around inside.

He had never been in an airplane before, but he was not afraid. He watched through the window as the motors were tested and the plane took off. When it sailed into the sky he looked back at the city where he was born, the only home he ever had known. Tears filled his eyes as he thought of his parents. When he looked down at the ocean, he could see the boats sailing on the water in the harbor. He was glad he was not on one of them.

The plane flew so high that it was above the clouds much of the time, and as Larry looked down he could see a white fluffy mass that reminded him of soapsuds on washday. For hours the ocean was hidden. But the clouds were beautiful. Some of them were so high that the plane flew through them, and he could see nothing outside but fog. Even the sun was shut out then. He was glad when he could see the blue sky above him once again.

At last he grew tired. The steward on the plane brought him a pillow and a blanket, lowered the back of his chair so that it was almost like a bed, and Larry went to sleep at the side of his missionary traveling companion. They flew all night, and Larry did not wake up until the plane landed at the big airport in New York.

There the missionary telephoned to the Jensens, telling them that he and Larry would arrive in Salt Lake City at seven o'clock the next morning. Paul and his parents were glad to receive this message.

10

That evening as Paul got ready for bed his mother talked with him in his bedroom for a while.

"Isn't it wonderful, Mother, that Larry is coming to live with us?" Paul said.

"Yes, it surely is," said Sister Jensen. "We hope that he will be happy here."

"I'll try to make him happy," said her young son. "We'll do everything together, and have lots of fun."

CHAPTER TWO

The Plane Arrives

Soon after daybreak the next morning Paul opened his eyes. It seemed as if he had dreamed all night long. As he lay there, slowly waking up, he began to wonder what Larry would look like. How tall was he? Was he fat or thin? Would they be in the same room in school? Could he ride a bike? What about baseball? Or did they play baseball in Denmark?

Paul remembered that he could not write Larry a letter because he didn't know Danish, and Larry could not read or speak English. How would the two boys talk together? This worried him.

His father softly opened the door and looked in. He saw his son lying there, his eyes wide open.

"Are you awake already, Paul?" he asked.

"Yes, Daddy. I woke up just a few minutes ago. Is it time to go to the plane?"

"Almost," said his father. "You'd better get up now."

Quick as a flash Paul hurried into the bathroom. He talked with his dad about Larry all the time he was washing and dressing.

His mother brought him a glass of juice, and explained

12

that they would all have breakfast together when they returned from the airport with Larry and the missionary. It would be Larry's first meal in his new home.

Paul sat between his mother and dad as they drove to the airport.

"Do they have bikes in Denmark, Mother?" he asked.

"Lots of them," replied his mother. "More than we have here. Nearly everyone rides bicycles in Denmark—boys and girls, fathers and mothers. They have as many bicycles there as we have automobiles in this country."

"Why?" he asked his mother, "don't they have any cars?"

"Not many. People over there can't afford automobiles," she explained. "And gasoline is scarce and very expensive. So they use bicycles.

"And do you know?" she went on, "I have seen some bicycles in Denmark that carried whole families. They had two seats and two sets of pedals and two handlebars, one for the father and the other for the mother. Then behind the mother was another seat for a child, and over the front handlebars was a seat for another child. So a family of four could ride on one bicycle at one time. It was very interesting to see. If there were more than two children, the older ones had another bicycle. So the whole family rode along and enjoyed it, just as we like to ride in our car."

He had never heard of anything like that before. Imagine, he thought to himself, a family without a car! But he did not know that there are many families who do not have cars, especially in other countries.

Perhaps Larry would tell him more about this, he thought. But then he remembered about the Danish language.

"Mother, how will I talk to Larry? He just speaks Danish?"

Sister Jensen smiled. She had thought of that too.

"I guess I'll have to do your talking for you until Larry learns English," she explained. "But it won't take him long. Youngsters learn new languages very fast."

Paul's father drove the car into a parking place near the airport building, and they all went inside. They walked to the waiting room where they watched for the plane which was due in ten minutes.

Paul couldn't sit still. He was too excited. He walked over to the large windows where he could see the planes outside, standing on the runways waiting to take off. He wondered where they were going, and how many people they could carry.

He saw one small plane coming down.

"Is that it, Mother?" he called out.

"No son," she said with a little laugh. "Larry's plane will be a big one."

Paul continued to watch. At the far end of the field he soon saw a large plane coming down for a landing.

"I think that's the one," said his dad. "Let's go outside."

They stood on the steps watching the huge ship as it roared up to the gates, where it stopped. Paul watched the men push toward the plane what looked like a little stairway on wheels which they placed against the door. The stewardess stepped out, followed by the passengers.

Some men came first, and then a little old lady. But where was Larry? More men came down the steps. Next a tall young man stepped out of the plane, holding the hand of a small boy about the size of Paul.

"Is that Larry?" asked Paul.

"I believe it is," replied his mother.

"Let's go out to meet them," urged Paul, tugging at her hand.

"We're not allowed to," she said. "We must wait here."

Brother Jensen waved to Larry and the missionary and they both waved back.

After coming through the gate the missionary shook hands with Brother and Sister Jensen and introduced himself as Elder Matheson. Then he shook hands with Paul, but Paul's eyes were on Larry, who stood behind Elder Matheson and seemed very quiet.

The missionary turned to Larry and took his hand.

"Now I want you to meet a wonderful Danish boy who has come to live with you," he said.

Although neither Paul nor his parents had seen Larry before, he already seemed like one of them. He felt strange

16

in this new land, but when Paul smiled at him, Larry smiled back. That was a language both could understand. Then Paul's Mother took Larry in her arms and with a hug such as only a mother can give, welcomed him to America and to their home. She spoke to him rapidly in Danish. Paul wondered what she was saying. As Larry listened, his face broke into a broad grin, so Paul knew he was happy.

Brother Jensen shook hands with Larry, and put his arm around his shoulder and pulled him close to him in a friendly, warm embrace. He smiled at Larry too. That was about all he could do because he couldn't speak any Danish either. Like Paul he would have to leave the talking to Sister Jensen for a while.

Paul's dad and Elder Matheson now walked out to the car, and Paul, his mother and Larry walked together behind. Sister Jensen and Larry were talking together constantly in Danish. Both laughed and seemed to have a good time.

Larry and Paul and his mother sat in the back seat of the car and Elder Matheson sat with Brother Jensen in front, as they drove home for breakfast.

Sister Jensen served them all Danish pan cakes and honey, with lots of nice cold milk. It reminded Larry of home.

CHAPTER THREE

Vacation Fun

Larry liked his new home in America. He liked Paul too, and enjoyed playing with him.

Paul had a dog named Jeff. He liked Larry and sat by his feet at supper time. At first Larry fed him scraps from his plate, but Paul's mother made him stop. Jeff must eat outside.

Larry soon learned to speak English. He became just like a little American boy. He rode Paul's bicycle and played ball with him. Soon he would have a bike of his own.

He went to school with Paul on week days, and to Sunday School on Sundays. He liked Sunday School. His teacher had been a missionary in Denmark, and sometimes he would say some Danish words to Larry which pleased him very much.

When school closed for the summer, Paul and Larry had their vacation. They liked to go to the canyon near their home with Jeff running alongside of them. They hiked up the hillside, and through the trees in the canyon, and they caught fish in the river.

Paul's father went with them on their fishing trips whenever he could leave his work. He was a good fisherman, and taught them how to fish. The boys dug worms for bait. Sometimes they did not use worms, when Brother Jensen brought fly hooks. He said they were better than worms.

One day as the boys were hiking in the canyon they saw a hole in the ground. It was almost big enough for Jeff to crawl into. Jeff smelled the hole, and began to bark loudly.

"There must be something inside," said Paul. "Dig for him, Jeffy, old boy. Dig."

Jeff dug and made the hole larger. Suddenly he howled, and backed away from it. As the dog drew back the boys saw the head of a strange looking animal.

"Get him, Jeff," cried out Paul. But Jeff was scared and ran off.

After the dog left, the animal came out of his hole and looked around. He walked toward the boys, and they became frightened and ran away as fast as they could.

When they reached home Paul told his dad about their adventure. As the boys described the animal he said, "O that was a badger."

He laughed when they told him how the badger had scared Jeff, but then he said, "Don't go near those holes any more. A badger could hurt you badly. They are hard fighters. One of them could kill Jeff."

Larry wanted to see Great Salt Lake. Paul had told him about it, and how much fun it was to swim there. Every summer the Jensens went to the lake for a swim. Larry asked if they would take him there some time.

Paul's mother promised the boys that they would all go next Saturday afternoon. Brother Jensen did not have to work on Saturday afternoons, and he could go with them. He liked swimming too.

It was a hot summer day when they went to the lake. They hurried into their swimming suits and waded out into the water. It felt nice and cool on such a hot day.

Brother Jensen took Larry by the hand, and Paul stayed close to his mother. They waded out far into the lake until the water came up to the boys' hips.

Brother Jensen told them that they must not splash in this water, because they might get some of it in their eyes.

20

The water was so salty that even a small drop in the eye would hurt badly.

"Would you like to float in this water?" Brother Jensen now asked Larry.

"Yes, I would," he said. "But don't let me go under."

Brother Jensen held Larry under each arm, and told him to let his feet come up. Larry was surprised as they floated right up to the surface.

"Now sit down in the water," said Brother Jensen, still holding to Larry's arms.

Larry sat down, just as though he were in a chair. He did not sink at all, but just sat there. He had never heard of water like this. When he had been swimming in the sea in Denmark, he would sink if he stopped swimming.

"Why don't I sink?" he asked.

"Because the water is full of salt," explained Brother Jensen.

"May I taste it?" Larry asked.

"Yes, if you are careful," said Brother Jensen. "Just put one finger in your mouth, but don't try to drink any. It would make you choke."

Larry put one finger in his mouth. Sure enough the water was very salty. Then he put another finger in. Now his mouth tasted so salty he wanted a drink of fresh water, but there wasn't any nearby.

"How would you like to float on your back?" Brother

Jensen asked. Larry said he would. Brother Jensen held his back carefully and Larry stretched out full length. He just lay there, without moving. Brother Jensen's hand was at his back, to keep him from turning over in the water, and getting his face in it. Larry just floated there. He was having a wonderful time. He laughed. He never had heard of this kind of swimming before.

Paul was floating too, his mother watching him.

When their swim was over, they waded back to the shore, and sat in the sun. In a few moments, the water dried and left white particles on their skin.

"Look," said Larry, "I'm all white."

"That's salt," said Brother Jensen. "Taste it and see."

Larry took some of the salt which had dried on his arm, and put it in his mouth. It was salt all right.

"Is it the kind of salt we eat on our food?" asked Larry.

"Yes, it is," said Sister Jensen. "On our way home we will drive over and show you the salt works where they clean the salt to use on the table."

After their showers in fresh water, they dried and dressed, and were ready for lunch. Their swim had given them a good appetite. They all went to the lunch stand and ate hot dogs. This was Larry's first hot dog. He had never seen one in Denmark. He was really enjoying his new experiences.

As they drove home, Brother Jensen turned the car off

on a side road, and went toward a large building. All around it were piles of white salt. They explained that water was pumped out of the lake upon little open spaces closed in by low walls. As the water dried in the hot sun, it left the salt behind. Then the salt was scraped together and was scooped into trucks and hauled to the mill where it was cleaned and put into boxes for sale in grocery stores.

"That is the way we get our salt," said Sister Jensen. "Isn't that interesting?"

"It surely is," said Larry. "We don't have anything like that in Denmark. I don't know where our salt came from."

CHAPTER FOUR

Riding Horseback

Paul had a cousin named Jim who lived on a farm. Paul told Larry about Jim, and about his horse Prince. Paul rode on Prince when he visited at Jim's house.

"Wouldn't you like to ride Prince?" Paul asked.

"I don't know," said Larry. "I have never been on a horse. I might fall off and get hurt."

"You wouldn't fall off Prince," said Paul. "He is too gentle."

At supper that night Paul asked his mother and father if they could all go out to Jim's place some time.

"That would be wonderful," said his mother. "His folks would like to see Larry. When can we go?" she asked her husband.

"What about next Saturday?" asked Brother Jensen. "That would be a good time for me."

"I will call Jim's mother on the phone and ask if they will be home," said Sister Jensen.

When she called, Jim's mother said they would be glad to see them. So it was arranged.

24

Early Saturday morning, they all got into the car and drove out to the ranch. They passed many farms on the way, some with cows in the pastures. As they drove along they came to a herd of sheep moving along the highway. They had to stop their car while the sheep passed by. A man on a horse, and two dogs were herding the sheep.

As they reached Jim's house, they drove into the driveway. Chickens ran away as they saw the car coming. Larry laughed to see them.

"They got out of their coop," said Brother Jensen. "We will have to tell Jim's dad about it."

Jim and his folks were at the door ready to greet them. They were so glad to see Larry, and shook him warmly by the hand. Jim was nine years old, two years older than Paul and Larry.

"Would you like to see my horse?" asked Jim.

"Yes, please," said Larry although he was a little afraid because he had not been around horses before.

"Will he kick?" he asked.

"Not Prince," said Jim.

"Will he bite?" again asked Larry, not too sure of getting very close to this horse. He had heard about horses biting people. The milk man at home had a horse once that bit a little girl who was trying to feed him.

"Naw," said Jim. "He never hurts anyone, you wait and see."

As they went out to the pasture Jim whistled, and Prince came on the run. He neighed softly at the boy as he drew near. Jim patted his nose and spoke to him.

"That's my Prince," he said. "Isn't he great?"

"He's wonderful," said Paul. "Are you going to let us have a ride?"

"Sure thing," said Jim. "Do you want to ride first?"

"You bet," said Paul. "I love to ride Prince."

"I'll have to get Dad to saddle him," he said. "Wait a minute, I'll be right back."

It was not long before the horse was ready to go. Jim pulled him close to the fence. Paul climbed up and stretched his right leg over the saddle. Soon he was sitting on Prince's back.

"Get up, Prince," he said, and Prince started off at a walk. He went all around the pasture and brought Paul back to where the other boys were waiting.

"Let me show you how to ride," said Jim. "Let me get on him."

Paul climbed back on to the fence, and then Jim mounted the horse. He was a good rider.

"Come on, Prince," he said, pulling on one of the lines. Prince started off at a trot this time, and was soon running fast around the pasture.

"Open the gate," called Jim.

Paul opened the gate, and Jim rode away on his beautiful horse. He galloped down the road for about a block, and then came back.

Larry watched him. It all looked so easy. He wondered if he could stay on Prince.

When Jim came back, he called out, "It's your turn now Larry," and pulled up at the side of the fence. Carefully he got down from the horse, and said, "Climb up, Larry."

Larry wanted to, but was still a little afraid.

"Don't be scared, he won't hurt you."

Carefully Larry climbed the fence, and slowly put one leg over the saddle, and pulled himself into place. He sat there for a moment, holding the saddle horn.

"You lead the horse for me, Jim," he said. "This is my very first ride."

Jim took the reins and slowly walked Prince part way down the road and back. It was fun, Larry told himself. Some day he would learn to ride, just like Jim.

CHAPTER FIVE

A Lesson Learned the Hard Way

One day Larry was riding Paul's bike in the street. He did not watch carefully. In making a quick turn he rode the bike into the side of an automobile and was knocked down.

The driver of the car stopped and called a policeman who took Larry to the hospital. He also called Paul's mother, and she and Paul hurried to Larry's bedside. The doctors found that Larry had broken his leg.

He was in great pain, and would have to stay in the hospital for at least a week. After that, the doctors had said he could go home.

He must wear a cast to keep the bone in place while it healed.

Brother Jensen visited Larry in the hospital. He told both Paul and Larry how careful they must be while riding the bicycle, because accidents do happen so easily. Both boys promised to more careful.

The doctor said that Larry could soon walk on crutches. Larry thought this would be fun. The nurse showed him how to use them. At first he could scarcely move, he was so afraid he would stumble and fall. But he tried a little each day, and soon could walk quite well. Then the doctor said he could leave the hospital.

When the Jensens came to bring him home, he was waiting at the door of his room, supporting himself with his crutches. A nurse brought a wheel chair, and wheeled him out to the car and they were soon driving away.

It felt good to be home again. Everyone was happy to see Larry back. Even Jeff barked and jumped and wagged his tail.

CHAPTER SIX

A Family Evening

Every week a family hour was held in Paul's home, and the boys looked forward to it. They always enjoyed the program, and especially the refreshments.

Soon after Larry came home from the hospital a family hour was held. Brother Jensen said, "We have something special to talk about tonight."

He told them that as soon as boys and girls in the Church are eight years old they should be baptized.

"What does it mean to be baptized?" asked Larry.

He had not been taught very much about the Church in Denmark, because his father did not have any religion.

"To be baptized," Brother Jensen went on, "is what we must do to become members of our Church."

"But we already go to Church," said Paul.

"Let me tell you a story," said his father, "to help you understand. You know when we are born into this world, we are all helpless little babies."

"Sure," said Paul.

"Have you ever wondered where we came from and

where we were before we were born as babies?" asked his dad.

"We came from heaven," said Larry. "My mother told me so."

"That's right, but where is heaven?"

The boys could not answer that one. They did not know. Brother Jensen then continued with his story.

"Heaven," he said, "is the place where God lives. God is our heavenly Father, and we were with him in his home before we were born here on this earth. It is very beautiful there. He has told us that if we keep his commandments while we are here on earth we can go back some time and live with him again. It is so wonderful there that we should do all we can to deserve this blessing.

"But we have to live really good lives, and as I said, we must become members of the Church too—Christ's own true Church."

"But Daddy," asked Paul, "there are lots of churches. Some of my friends at school belong to them. Are they all the same? Why are there so many of them?"

"Those are good questions," said his father. "Let me try to tell you about it. Those churches are not all the same. They are very different indeed.

"You remember that a few minutes ago I asked you where we lived before we were born here on earth."

"Yes," said Paul.

"And we said we lived in heaven and that God is our Father. Every one on earth is a child of God," said Brother Jensen. "We all lived together with Him in heaven as one big family."

"Where is heaven, Daddy?" asked Paul.

"Come outside with me for a minute," said his father.

CHAPTER SEVEN

A Lesson About Stars

They all went outside the house. It was a beautiful clear night. The stars were shining and there was a half moon.

"Just a moment," said Brother Jensen, "I have forgotten something."

He went back into the house and soon brought his big field glasses, the ones he took with him when he went deer hunting.

"I'm glad it's such a clear night," he said. "I want you to look at the sky with these glasses.

He pointed the glasses at the moon, and looked carefully. Then he passed them on to his wife. She looked for what the boys thought was a very long time. They waited impatiently for a chance to look through them.

"I had no idea these glasses would make such a difference," she said.

Each boy now had a turn. The moon looked much bigger and brighter to them through the glasses.

"Now look at that bright star," said Brother Jensen, as Larry was staring through the glasses.

At first Larry couldn't find the star in the glasses, but

with a little help he pointed them toward the right place. Even this star looked bigger and brighter.

Then Paul had his turn looking at the star, and he also was surprised at the way the glasses seemed to magnify and enlarge it.

"Now," said his dad. "Put down the glasses. I want you to see something else."

He pointed out one long streak of light in the sky in which there were many stars.

"That is the Milky Way," he said.

"Why do they call it that?" asked Paul.

"Because so much light comes from the many stars there that the sky looks white. That's why it is called the Milky Way."

"There are so many stars in the sky that no one can count them," said Paul's mother. "Most of them are bigger than our earth—even larger than our sun which is many times larger than the earth."

"That's right," said Brother Jensen, "and our Father in Heaven made them all."

"Does he live on one of them?" now asked Larry.

"He surely does," said Brother Jensen. "He lives on the most wonderful star in the sky, and he takes care of all the others from there."

"You should take the boys to look through the University telescope some night," said Sister Jensen. "They could see something really interesting there."

"I'll do that mother, first chance I get," he said, as they walked slowly inside the house.

CHAPTER EIGHT

Our Great Teacher

They sat down in the living room, and Brother Jensen continued his story.

"While we were all living with our Father in his heavenly home, he called us together to talk with us. He told us that he would prepare an earth—this one on which we are living—and that we could have it for our home.

"He said we would have parents here and would be born as babies to them. That is how we came to be born in our homes here on earth.

"But he also told us that we must live good lives while we are here if we wished to come back into his presence, because no unclean thing can be in heaven.

"He knew that we would need a great teacher to show us the way to live so that we could come back to our heavenly home. So he gave us his oldest Son in heaven as our teacher. He was called Jehovah in that heavenly home, but when he was born as a little baby in Bethlehem, he was called Jesus. He became our Savior.

"When Jesus was born on the first Christmas, the heavenly hosts sang for joy.

"He lived as a boy near Jerusalem in the city of Nazareth. When he became a man he went to the River Jordan where John the Baptist was baptizing the people, and asked to be baptized. Jesus said it must be done to 'fulfill all righteousness,' so John baptized him.

"This was one of the first things he did to show us how to live here on earth. He expects all of us to be baptized, just as he was.

"Later he organized his Church, with Twelve Apostles to help him with his work."

CHAPTER NINE

The Church Was Taken Away

"The Church which Jesus organized was a guide to mankind, to show them how to live in the way Jesus wants people to live.

"After Jesus finished his work here on earth he went back to our Father, to live with him in heaven. Then his twelve Apostles became the leaders of the Church. But wicked men began to fight against them. They killed the apostles and many members of the Church. At last the Lord took the Church away from the earth, because men were too wicked in those days for the pure Church of God to stay among them.

"Later other men tried to make churches of their own. But they did not understand the gospel. Many men made churches of their own, each using his own ideas and teachings. The Lord did not guide them, so they made many mistakes. That is why there are so many different churches in the world today.

"More than a hundred years ago, the boy Joseph Smith, then only 14 years old, wanted to know which of the many churches was the right one.

41

"He read in the Bible that if we need help, we should pray to the Lord, and if we ask in faith, we will receive an answer to our prayers.

"He went out into a grove of trees near his home and knelt there to pray, asking the Lord to tell him which of all these churches he should join.

"In answer to his prayer, our Heavenly Father and Jesus, his Beloved Son, came to him, in that grove.

"Jesus told Joseph not to join any of them, because they had been made by men who did not follow the teachings of the Lord.

"Joseph was told that if he would live a good life, the Lord would give him more help when he grew a little older.

"Three years went by. Now Joseph was seventeen. One night as he was praying before going to bed, he noticed that his room was growing light.

"In the light stood an angel from heaven, who said that his name was Moroni, and that he had lived in America hundreds of years ago.

"Moroni said that Joseph had been chosen by the Lord to receive an ancient record called the Book of Mormon. It was a sacred history of early America, engraved on plates of gold.

"The ancient Americans were the forefathers of the Indians of today. They came from Jerusalem. Prophets led them to America.

"Moroni told Joseph Smith that the gold plates on which this book was written were hidden in a hill not far from his home.

"Next day Joseph met Moroni on this hill, and Moroni showed him where the plates were. Joseph pried off the rock covering, and saw under it a stone box, inside of which were these plates of gold. The hill in which the plates were found was called Cumorah.

"Moroni told Joseph he could not take the plates for four

more years. Every year for those four years, Joseph met Moroni in the same place, and received instructions from him. On the last visit to the hill, Moroni let him take the plates.

"Through the help of the Lord, Joseph wrote the book in our language and published it. That is how we got the Book of Mormon."

CHAPTER TEN

Joseph Smith Is Baptized

Larry and Paul listened carefully to Brother Jensen. Larry had never heard this story before. His father had not liked the missionaries in Denmark, so they were not able to tell him of the gospel. He was very interested.

"Would you like to hear more of this story?" Brother Jensen asked, "or have we talked enough for one night?"

"Please tell us more, Uncle Fred," asked Larry. "It makes me feel so good inside."

"All right," said Brother Jensen. "I will. The Lord knew that Joseph Smith would need some one to help him with the printing of the Book of Mormon, so he sent several men to him. One of these was a school teacher whose name was Oliver Cowdery.

"One day when these two young men were working on the book, they read about baptism. They did not understand it, so they decided to ask the Lord.

"As they knelt in prayer, another angel came to them. He was John the Baptist, who had baptized Jesus.

"John ordained them to the Aaronic Priesthood, which has the power to baptize. It was the same priesthood he held himself. After he had given them this heavenly power, he told them to use it by baptizing each other. No one may baptize without this authority or priesthood which John gave to Joseph and Oliver.

"About a month later, Peter, James and John, the ancient apostles of the Lord, came to Joseph and Oliver, and gave them the higher priesthood, and the power to organize the true Church of Jesus Christ on earth again."

"Did Joseph and Oliver have to be baptized, Daddy?" Paul now asked.

"Yes, they did," replied his father. "As I told you, John told them to baptize each other, and that is what they did."

"Is that the way they joined the true Church?" Larry asked.

46

"That is right," said Brother Jensen, "and that is the way everyone must join it."

"Were you and Mother baptized?" Paul asked.

"Yes, we were, when we were eight years old," he replied. "And you boys may be baptized when you are eight, too."

"That's fine, Dad!" said Paul. "We'd like it, wouldn't we Larry?"

"Yes, but how is it done?" asked Larry anxiously.

He was afraid of new things, and baptism was very new to him.

"Larry," said Brother Jensen in a kindly voice, "your mother taught you about Jesus didn't she?"

"Yes, she did, Uncle Fred," he said, "and I believe in him. If we have to be baptized to be with him, then I want to be baptized."

"Tell us how it is done," said Paul.

CHAPTER ELEVEN

The Only Way

Brother Jensen was happy that the boys were so interested. He explained to them just what is done.

"First of all we will go with you to see our bishop," he said. "He will ask you if you want to be baptized and if you are good boys. Then he will give each of you a little printed piece of paper called a recommend which he signs, showing that you are ready.

"On the Saturday before Fast Day we will go to the Tabernacle where there is a small pool of water called a font. There are also some dressing rooms there.

"You boys will dress in white and so will I, because I will ask permission to baptize you myself.

"I will take each of you, one at a time, into the font and there in the name of Jesus I will baptize you by lowering you quickly but gently into the water, and taking you out again just as quickly. You will need to hold your breath for only a second or two.

"I will do Paul first, so that Larry can see how it is done. Then I will baptize Larry."

"Fine, Dad," Paul said again. "But why do we have to be put under the water like that?"

"There is a good reason for that," said his Dad. "It is to help us remember the death and resurrection of Jesus.

"When he died, he was put in a tomb or grave. When he was resurrected he came up out of his grave.

"We are buried in the water to remind us of his burial in the grave. We come up out of the water to remind us of the way Jesus came out of his grave to eternal life.

"There is something else about baptism we should mention here," said Brother Jensen. "In baptism we promise the Lord that we will serve him all the rest of our lives. So you see it is very important.

"The Lord gave us the Church to guide us in living right, and baptism makes us members of the Church."

"But why do we have to join it, Dad? I don't understand it yet," said Paul.

"Let us take Larry's life as an example," went on his father. "He lives in America now, and enjoys it, don't you Larry?"

"Yes, I do," he said. "And I don't ever want to leave here."

"That's right," said Brother Jensen. "It is wonderful to live in this country. But if we never came here we could never enjoy being here, could we?

"If Larry had stayed in Denmark, he would always have

50

been a Danish boy, wouldn't he? He had to come to America and live with us, and be a part of our family, in our house, before he could be an American boy. Isn't that right?"

Paul nodded his head. Larry just stared into his uncle's face. But there was a light in his eyes. He could understand this, even better than Paul.

"It is the same with the Church," Brother Jensen went on. "We might say that the Church is a house—the House of God, and all who are in it belong to the family of God, just as we here in this house all belong to one family.

"Since Larry could not be an American boy without coming here and joining an American family, so we cannot be members of the family of God unless we enter his house, or join his Church. And baptism is the way we enter. It is the door."

CHAPTER TWELVE

How We Must Live

"What do we have to do after we join the Church?" Paul asked his father.

"Just go on living very much as we do now," said his Dad. "You are already living the gospel, because that is the way we all live here in our family.

"If you had been born in another family where the gospel was not lived at home, you would have to change your ways and do what the Lord commands. But we here in our family are trying to do that now. We might mention a few things any way, just as a reminder.

"Baptized boys and girls should always treat everyone right. They should treat others as they would like to be treated themselves.

"They should not lie, or cheat, or gossip about their friends. They should never steal, and they should never swear, because the name of God is sacred.

"The Lord teaches us to honor our parents. This means being kind to them, and doing what they tell us to do, not making a lot of excuses.

"The Lord expects us to keep the Sabbath Day, too. We

must go to our meetings every Sunday, and be quiet and listen to the teacher, and learn all we can.

"Whenever we receive any money, we should pay our tithing to the bishop."

"What is tithing?" asked Larry. This too was something about which he had never heard.

"When we pay tithing," his uncle explained, "we give to the bishop, who is the Lord's servant, a tenth of all the money we receive. In Primary I learned to say this:

> I know what tithing is,
> I'll tell you every time;
> Ten cents from a dollar,
> And a penny from a dime.

"If we earn ten cents for helping someone, we should pay the bishop one penny of it. We can keep the other nine pennies for ourselves. Or if we earn a dollar, we should pay him a dime.

"That isn't very much, is it, because if the Lord lets us keep nine cents out of every ten, we should be willing to give him just one, shouldn't we? He gives us nine times as much as he asks for himself.

"That shows in only one way how kind the Lord is to his children. For everything else we do in obeying him, he repays us many times over.

"To receive his blessings we must live near to him, and talk with him. This we do in prayer. Every one of us should pray at least twice a day, morning and night, and at other times too when we need to.

"The Lord teaches us to ask for what we need, and to ask it of our Father in Heaven. Jesus taught us to pray, beginning with the words: 'Our Father which art in Heaven, hallowed be thy name.'

"All our prayers must be to our Father. We do not pray to Jesus, nor to any one else, only to our Father in Heaven.

"As we pray to him, we may ask for whatever we need. But we should not ask the Lord to do something which we can do for ourselves. He expects us to do all we can for ourselves.

"When we have finished our prayer we should always end it with the words, 'In the name of Jesus Christ, Amen.' "

Paul's mother now spoke up and said, "But there is more to prayer than just asking for things. We must always remember to thank the Lord for what we have and for all the thing he does for us every day."

"That's right, Mother," said Brother Jensen. "I am so glad you spoke of that. The Lord expects us to be thankful for our blessings."

CHAPTER THIRTEEN

Forgiveness of Sin

Sister Jensen had not said much during the evening, but when prayer was spoken of she joined in the conversation.

"When Jesus was on earth," she said, "he prayed to his Father very often. He also taught the people to pray. As he did so, he told them to ask the Lord to forgive them of the wrong things they did.

"This refers to baptism too," she said. "Daddy, tell the boys about forgiveness of sin."

"I will be glad to," he said. "It surely is a part of baptism.

"When older people join the Church, they also must learn to live right. They may have many habits which are not good, just as some children do. They must change them, and begin living right.

"They know that when they sin they displease God. They ask his forgiveness. Forgiveness means that the Lord will not hold our sins against us if we stop doing the things that are wrong.

"When an older person joins the Church, he is baptized just like you boys will be, and then, the Lord forgives him of his sins, if he stops doing wrong. It is in baptism that God grants this forgiveness. That is why it is spoken of as baptism for the remission of sins.

"We must be clean and free from sin when joining the Church, for no unclean person can come into God's house.

"We all have done things that are wrong, and I guess we will do more in the future. But we must always try to do better.

"Now you boys think of the bad habits you may have, and then try to overcome them before you are baptized, so that you will be forgiven by the Lord as you come up out of the water."

Paul spoke up now. He had an idea.

"I know one thing I will change," he said. "I always throw rocks at Anderson's cat. I'll stop doing that."

"And I won't come in the house with muddy feet any more," said Larry.

"And I will come when you call me, Mother," said Paul.

"And I will feed Jeff outside, and not at the table," said Larry.

"That's right boys," said Brother Jensen. "Think of all the bad habits you can remember. One of the best things you can do is to keep the Golden Rule, and treat other people as you would like them to treat you.

"When you are about to do something unkind to one of your friends, just ask yourself if you would like him to do it to you. If you would not like it, you can be sure he wouldn't like it either. In this way you may know it is wrong."

Mother looked at the clock. It was a quarter to nine.

"O," she said. "It's late—past your bedtime."

"That's right," said Brother Jensen, "but we've had a good time."

"Yes," said Paul, "but not good enough."

"Not good enough, Paul?" asked his mother. "Haven't you enjoyed what your Dad has been telling us?"

"Sure," he said, "but where are the refreshments? It isn't a home evening without a treat, is it?"

Mother and Dad looked at each other, and laughed.

"All right, you win," said Sister Jensen. "I really forgot it."

Ice cream and cake—the boys' favorite. They all laughed and talked as they ate. Then both boys went to bed.

As they were getting into their pajamas, Larry said, "Paul I'm so glad I'm an American boy now, and I'm so glad I can be baptized."

Then he paused for a moment, and said, "I wonder if I'll still have this cast on my leg on my birthday."

Chapter Fourteen

Baptism of the Spirit

The boys looked forward to their birthdays. Paul's came on October 15 and Larry's on October 29.

The regular day for baptism was the Saturday before Fast Day. Both boys were to be baptized on the same day, and they would then be confirmed together too.

As they listened to Paul's parents talking about being confirmed, Larry was puzzled.

"What does it mean to be confirmed?" he asked.

"In our next family hour, we will explain," Sister Jensen said.

Paul had seen people confirmed at fast meeting, but this was all new to Larry. He hadn't heard about any of these things in Denmark. The missionaries had visited his home but his dad was not interested in what they said. His mother had believed them, but never was baptized because her husband did not approve.

Friday night was chosen as home evening this week. Paul and Larry prepared games and Sister Jensen made a sponge cake.

They all enjoyed the games and then sat quietly while

Brother Jensen gave the lesson. As Sister Jensen had promised it was on being confirmed a member of the Church.

"You remember," said Brother Jensen, "that last week we talked about baptism. We told you only a part of the story.

"There are two parts to baptism. One is called baptism in water, and that is what we told you about last week. The other is called baptism of the Spirit.

"Listen carefully while I explain this, as it is very important. When we repent of our sins, we receive forgiveness of them in the waters of baptism. That makes us clean in the sight of God.

"He has told us that if we do what is right our bodies may be a dwelling place for his Spirit, which really comes upon us.

"But he says that his Spirit will not enter an unclean tabernacle or house. He speaks of our bodies as tabernacles, or dwelling places for his Holy Spirit.

"As we are cleansed of sin in the waters of baptism, we are made ready to receive his Spirit.

"The way we receive his Holy Spirit is that the elders of the Church lay their hands upon our heads, after we are baptized in water, and bless us and say, 'Receive the Holy Ghost.'

"Then the Holy Spirit does come upon us, and helps us to purify our souls and minds. As long as we live according to the Lord's teachings it will remain with us, and will prompt us to do right.

"If we do wrong, we drive the Holy Spirit away from us. Our sinful acts offend the Spirit, and it draws away from us and no longer helps us.

"So you see why we need to live right every day.

"When the elders say, 'Receive the Holy Ghost,' we do receive it as a gift from our Father in Heaven, and it is spoken of in the Church as the Gift of the Holy Ghost.

"Not only do the elders give us this gift, but they also say, 'We confirm you a member of the Church of Jesus Christ of Latter-day Saints.'

"So that you will understand what that means let me explain that after we have received the two kinds of baptism —first in water and then the baptism of the Holy Ghost—we are ready to have our names placed on the records of the Church.

"When the elders say 'we confirm you a member of the Church' it puts the stamp of approval by the priesthood upon all that has been done. It also makes it possible for the bishop to write our names on the Church records as members of the Church. That is what it means to be confirmed.

CHAPTER FIFTEEN

Birthday Parties

Sister Jensen planned birthday parties for both boys. When she asked Paul what kind of party he would like, he said, "A roller skating party."

When she asked Larry about his, the Danish boy said, "A hot-dog and doughnut party."

The Jensens gave both boys what they asked for.

After the roller skating party Paul brought his friends home for cake and ice cream, his favorite dessert. Everyone had a good time.

When Larry's birthday came around, the Jensens gave him a sled for coasting in the winter, which made him very happy. There had been snow in Denmark, but no coasting.

He wanted to see where people went coasting in the winter, and Paul and his father took him in the car to show him. There were two hills in the city where children were allowed to coast but they were small. Paul wanted to show Larry a place in Emigration Canyon where his parents took him last winter.

Larry was really impressed when he saw that hill.

As they drove back toward home, Larry said, "Are we

still going to have hot dogs and doughnuts? Do you think your mother remembered, Paul?"

"Mother? She never forgets anything," said Paul.

It was dark when they reached home. As the boys entered the house, Sister Jensen asked them to go into the living room. Larry led the way. He could smell those hot dogs and doughnuts.

The lights had not been turned on in the front room, so he felt for the switch. As he pressed it, and the lights came on, he saw that the room was filled with young people. They shouted loudly, "Surprise!"

It was Larry's first surprise party. They all had a good time, playing games and singing. Then came the refreshments, the hot dogs and doughnuts and cider, all they could eat and drink.

Brother Jensen served the food. He dressed up like a cook, with a white apron and a tall white cap. Sister Jensen brought in the cider.

Larry felt that he had never had such a good time. The Jensens were certainly good to him, he thought. That night, as he thanked them for the wonderful party and the sled, he asked them if there was something he could do to really thank them for all they had done for him.

Sister Jensen took him in her arms and said, "Just keep on loving us—and be a good boy—that will be thanks enough."

CHAPTER SIXTEEN

The Boys Are Baptized

Early Saturday morning following Larry's birthday party, the family got ready to go to the Tabernacle. It was the day the boys were to be baptized.

As they reached the Tabernacle they were shown to the dressing rooms where they were given white clothes. Brother Jensen was with them. He had been given permission to baptize them.

They went into the large room where other children were waiting their turn to be baptized. In the front of the room was the font. It was large and beautiful, made of gleaming white tile.

They sat down and waited for the services to begin. Soon one of the brethren called the meeting to order. A song was sung and a prayer was given. Then the baptisms began. The boys watched with much interest.

"I'm not afraid of that," said Larry. "When will it be our turn?"

"In a few moments," said his uncle. "They will call our names."

More boys and girls were baptized, and then Paul and
Larry were called.

Brother Jensen led the boys to the edge of the font, then
he and Paul walked down the little stairway into the water.

The water was warm and not very deep. His father held

Paul's hands in his own left one. He raised his right hand and said:

"Paul Jensen, having been commissioned of Jesus Christ I baptize you in the name of the Father and of the Son and of the Holy Ghost. Amen."

Then he placed his right hand on Paul's back, between the shoulders, and lowered him into the water, and quickly raised him up again.

Paul hurried up the steps and ran to the dressing room for his towel.

Larry, now free from his cast, and quite able to walk, stepped down into the water and took his uncle's hand. Brother Jensen smiled at him and Larry smiled back. He wasn't afraid now. He wondered why he had been afraid before. But that was when he knew nothing about baptism and had not seen it performed.

He took a deep breath as his uncle spoke the words of the ceremony, and held his breath as he was lowered into the water. Then his uncle lifted him up, and helped him to the stairs.

"It was easy," he whispered to his uncle. "I liked it."

Next day was Fast Day. The ward fast meeting was held soon after Sunday School.

There were several babies to be blessed and two other children to be confirmed, in addition to Paul and Larry.

Larry watched closely. When Paul was called he went

70

to the front of the chapel and sat on a chair in front of the first bench. His father went with him.

The bishopric and Brother Jensen all laid their hands on Paul's head and confirmed him a member of the Church and said to him: "Receive the Holy Ghost."

Larry was called next and he went forward and received the same blessings.

As the boys walked home with Brother and Sister Jensen, Paul said, "Well, Larry how do you feel?"

"Great," said the little orphan boy. "I feel like I really belong to you folks now—and to the Lord."